Early TOY Encyclopedias

LEGO

by Ryan Gale

Early Encyclopedias

An Imprint of Abdo Reference

abdobooks.com

abdobooks.com

Published by Abdo Reference, a division of ABDO, PO Box 398166, Minneapolis, Minnesota 55439.

Printed in China.
052025
092025

THIS BOOK CONTAINS RECYCLED MATERIALS

Editor: Haley Williams
Series Designers: Candice Keimig, Joshua Olson
Production Designer: Ryan Gale

Library of Congress Control Number: 2024949006

Publisher's Cataloging-in-Publication Data

Names: Gale, Ryan, author.
Title: Lego / by Ryan Gale
Description: Minneapolis, Minnesota: Abdo Reference, 2026 | Series: Early toy encyclopedias | Includes online resources and index.
Identifiers: ISBN 9781098297565 (lib. bdg.) | ISBN 9798384930082 (ebook)
Subjects: LCSH: LEGO toys--Juvenile literature. | Blocks (Toys)--Juvenile literature. | Toys--Juvenile literature. | Popular culture--Juvenile literature. | Collectibles--Juvenile literature. | Reference materials--Juvenile literature. | Encyclopedias and dictionaries--Juvenile literature.
Classification: DDC 688.725--dc23

CONTENTS

INTRODUCTION

Since 1958, Lego bricks have come out in about 200 different colors.

Lego Bricks

Lego bricks are among the most popular toys of all time. The bricks are made of colored plastic. They connect to each other. They are used to make buildings, vehicles, and more. Lego bricks are meant for boys and girls. Many adults enjoy them too.

FUN FACT!

Lego bricks were named Toy of the Century by *Fortune* magazine in 2000.

Sets

Lego bricks come in sets. Most sets have instructions. The instructions show people how to build each set. People can also build things from their imaginations. Builds can be taken apart. The bricks can be reused to make other things.

People of all ages can play with Legos.

FUN FACT!

The Lego Group stopped making wooden toys in 1960.

A Danish Toymaker

Lego bricks are made by the Lego Group. The company is based in Billund, Denmark. It was started by Ole Kirk Kristiansen. He made furniture. He also made wooden toys. Kristiansen named his toy company Lego in 1936. Lego is short for *leg godt*. It means "play well" in Danish.

A wooden duck is one of the most famous early toys created by Lego.

Ole Kirk Kristiansen, *right*, and his son, Godtfred, *left*, worked together at the Lego Group.

Automatic Binding Bricks

Kristiansen saw a set of plastic bricks in 1947. They were called Self-Locking Building Bricks. They were made by the British toy company Kiddicraft. Kristiansen began making similar plastic bricks in 1949. He called them Automatic Binding Bricks. The name was changed to Lego Bricks in 1953.

Buildings in the Town Plan set included a fire station, church, and store.

The Lego System in Play

The Lego System in Play was created in 1955. All Lego pieces in the System fit together. The more pieces people had, the more things they could build. The first Lego System set came out in 1955. It was called Town Plan. The set featured buildings and roads.

Studs and Tubes

The first Lego bricks were hollow inside. They had studs on top. The studs allowed bricks to fit together. But the bricks came apart too easily. Hollow tubes were added inside the bricks in 1958. The studs fit tightly into the tubes. This helped the bricks stick together better.

The Lego Group's stud and tube design was patented in 1958.

Minifigures

The first Lego figures came out in 1975. They did not have arms or legs. The heads did not have faces. They were also yellow. Yellow was a neutral color. It did not stand for any one skin color. Figures with movable arms and legs were made in 1978. They had smiley faces. The Lego Group called them minifigures, or minifigs.

Evolution of the Minifigure

Lego figures have changed over time to include different faces and skin colors.

Armless minifigure (1975)

Classic minifigure (1978)

New faces (1989)

Short legs (2002)

Realistic skin tones (2003)

Mini-doll (2012)

Baby minifigure (2016)

Set Number

Each Lego set has a set number. This makes it easier for people to search for the set online.

Themes

In 1978, the Lego Group sorted its sets into themes. The first themes were Castle, Town, and Space. They represented the past, present, and future. More themes were added over time. They began including action and story elements.

Where to Find Lego Sets

Lego sets are sold in most toy stores. Other stores may also sell Lego sets. New and old sets can be bought online.

Legoland Theme Parks

More than 16 million people visited the Legoland theme parks in 2023.

Expansion

The Lego Group built on the success of its bricks. It made Lego books, comics, and video games. A Legoland theme park opened in Billund in 1968. By 2024, there were ten parks worldwide. Millions of people visit the parks each year.

Movies and Television

The Lego Group began releasing movies on home video in 2003. Then *The Lego Movie* came out in 2014. It was the first Lego movie released in theaters. *The Lego Movie 2* released five years later. Many animated television shows have also been made. The reality show *Lego Masters* came out in 2020. People compete to be the best Lego builder.

Emmet, *middle*, is the main character of *The Lego Movie*.

Lego Designers

Teams of designers create Lego sets. Some designers work from drawings or photographs. Ideas also come from designers' imaginations. The finished sets are then reviewed. Once approved, the sets are made in the Lego Group's factories.

Lego designers help create the pieces and instructions that go into each set.

Robots help produce, organize, and transport Lego pieces in factories.

Making Bricks

Lego factories use machines to make the bricks. The machines melt colored plastic. The plastic is poured into molds. These molds have hollow spaces in the shape of bricks. The melted plastic fills the spaces and takes the shape of the bricks. The plastic hardens as it cools. Then the bricks are removed from the molds.

FUN FACT!

Factories make about 36,000 Lego pieces every minute.

There are more than 1,000 Lego stores worldwide.

Assembly

Some Lego pieces are assembled before being sold. Machines add hands to arms and attach the arms to minifigure bodies. Other machines use stamps. They place images on some Lego parts. Finished bricks are packaged into sets. The sets are shipped around the world.

Evolution of the Lego Logo

The logo for the Lego Group has changed several times over its history.

1934

1946

1950

1953

1955

1956

1958

1964

1972

Basic

Early Lego sets included basic bricks. The boxes had images of things that could be built. But there were no instructions. Children would build using their imaginations. These types of sets were later called Basic. The Basic line was renamed Classic in 2015.

Basic sets came with simple pieces that allowed kids to build different things.

The garage door in the 1955 Garage and Van set could open and close.

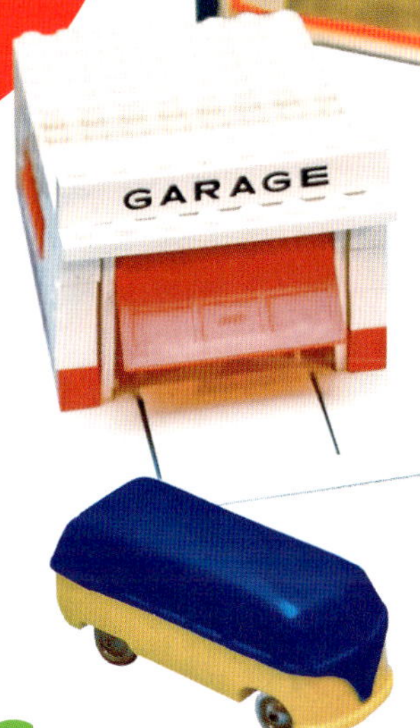

Early Sets

In the 1950s, Lego released sets that built specific things. They had building instructions on the boxes. Sets featured things children saw every day. These included buildings, cars, and trucks. Separate instruction books were introduced in 1963.

Top Five Largest Lego Sets

This chart shows the top five largest Lego sets by number of pieces.

SET NAME	NUMBER OF PIECES	YEAR RELEASED
LEGO ART WORLD MAP*	11,695	2021
LEGO ICONS EIFFEL TOWER	10,001	2022
LEGO ICONS *TITANIC*	9,090	2021
LEGO COLOSSEUM*	9,036	2020
UCS LEGO STAR WARS *MILLENNIUM FALCON*	7,541	2017

*Retired set

Legos in the United States

Lego bricks were sold only in Europe until 1961. That year, Lego made a deal with the luggage company Samsonite. The deal let Samsonite sell Lego sets in the United States. These sets were called Lego System. The Lego Group ended the deal in 1972. It began selling its own products in the United States.

Enfield Office

The Lego Group opened its first US office in 1975. It was located in Enfield, Connecticut. In 2023, the company announced it was closing the Enfield office. The new office would be in Boston, Massachusetts.

Early Lego sets were marketed only to children.

Duplo

Lego Duplo bricks were first made in 1969. The bricks are meant for children one to four years old. They are twice the size of System bricks. The large size makes it harder for young children to choke on them. Duplo and System bricks fit together even though they are different sizes.

Duplo figures have movable arms and legs. They also have more realistic features compared to those of Lego minifigures.

Duplo sets have many themes, such as Cars, Dino, and Farm.

Duplo Sets

There are many types of Duplo sets. Some have only basic bricks. Others have bricks with numbers. Those help children learn to count. There are sets for making cars, trains, and boats. Some Duplo sets have characters from movies and TV.

FUN FACT!

Some early Lego sets came with plastic toy cars.

TOWN/CITY THEME

The Town Square-Castle Scene was an early set from the Town theme.

Legoland Town

Legoland Town was one of the first Lego themes. It was introduced in 1978. The Town theme featured things from the real world. These included buildings and vehicles.

Baseplates

Baseplates are flat plates. They have studs for attaching bricks. They are used as bases to build on. Baseplates come in many sizes and colors. Some have smooth roads and rivers. Others have raised hills and ramps. Some have printed designs. These include sand, stone, and water.

Green is one of the most common baseplate colors.

Police

Police sets are a popular part of the Town theme. These sets often feature police stations, cars, and helicopters. The first police set was the 1972 Police Heliport. There have been many police minifigures. The first criminal minifig came out in 1993.

The Lego Group has sold several police chase sets.

The Lego Fire House set came out in 1973. It featured three fire vehicles, one of which had a ladder.

Fire

The Town theme has also featured many firefighter sets. Sets often include fire stations, trucks, and boats. The first set was the 1957 Lego Fire Station. Fire sets changed over time. They began including more firefighting action. They also added see-through flames and water pieces.

Lights and Sounds

Some Lego sets have lights and sounds. Light-up bricks first came out in 1957. Lights and sounds are often used in police and fire sets.

The 1961 airplane set had instructions for building several types of planes.

Flight

Lego began selling airplane sets in the early 1960s. Flight became a Town subtheme in 1985. It featured sets with airplanes, helicopters, and space shuttles. Lego also sold sets based on real airplanes.

FUN FACT!

Retired Lego sets are sets that are no longer sold by the Lego Group.

Airports

There have been many Lego airport sets over the years. The first was the 1970 Mini-Airport and Vehicles set. Airport sets often come with airplanes. They may also have vehicles. These include luggage cars and fuel trucks.

The 1985 Airport was one of the first sets where minifigures could fit in the body of the airplane.

Trains

Trains are popular with many Lego builders. The first Lego train set was released in 1964. The first battery-powered Lego train came out the year after. Trains was a separate theme from 1980 to 2003. Then it became part of the Lego World City line. Some sets include train stations.

People can change the design or length of Lego train tracks.

Nautica was a Town subtheme that released in 1991. It included five sets.

Ships

Several Lego ship sets have released over time. These include rescue, exploration, and cargo ships. Some sets have ports. This is where ships dock to load cargo and passengers.

The Lego Separator

The Lego Separator tool came out in 1990. It is used to separate Legos that can be hard to take apart by hand. Separators are usually included in large sets.

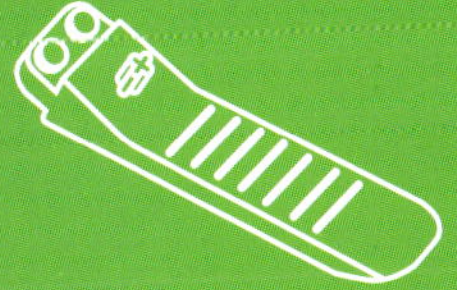

The 2013 Lego City Race Car featured a minifigure with a trophy.

Racing

Race cars have been a part of the Town theme since the early 1970s. Some race cars are remote-controlled. The 1998 Radio Control Racer was the first remote-controlled Lego vehicle. Lego Racers was its own theme from 2001 to 2012. Some sets were models of real-life cars. These included cars from Ferrari and Lamborghini.

FUN FACT!

Octan is a fictional gas company created by the Lego Group for the Town/ City theme.

Speed Champions

Speed Champions is an ongoing theme. It began in 2015. Sets feature more realistic race cars. The cars are very detailed. They are meant for adults.

Lego Tires

The Lego Group began making tires in the early 1960s. The tires allowed builders to make vehicles that could roll. The company makes about 306 million tires every year.

Speed Champions features race cars from companies such as Ferrari, Porsche, and Aston Martin.

The 1990 Space Shuttle had 392 pieces and included three minifigures.

Space Exploration

In 1990, Lego came out with a National Aeronautics and Space Administration (NASA) space shuttle. NASA is the US government's space program. The shuttle set was part of the Town theme.

Mission to Mars

Other Town/City space sets followed. In 2019, the City theme had sets about missions to Mars. These sets included rockets, shuttles, and rovers. City space sets came with alien figures in 2024.

Parts of the 2019 Mars Research Shuttle set were inspired by real NASA technology.

Paradisa

Paradisa was a series of Town sets marketed toward girls. Sets had beach vacation and horse-riding themes. The minifigs were mostly female. Bricks came in colors such as pink and light green. Eighteen Paradisa sets were released between 1992 and 1997.

Female minifigs in the Paradisa series had either eyelashes and red lips or freckles.

The Lego Group expanded the City theme to include construction and emergency vehicle sets.

Lego City

The Town theme was renamed City Center in the United States. This was from 1999 to 2000. It was renamed City in Europe. The theme had larger and more complex sets. It was rebranded as Lego World City from 2003 to 2004. The name was shortened to just City in 2005.

The 2015 Deep Sea Exploration Vessel included a shipwreck, submarine, and shark cage.

Exploration

Some sets went beyond towns and cities. The 1997 Town Divers sets explored the ocean. They featured submarines, sea creatures, and ships. Other exploration themes included Arctic and Volcano Explorers.

National Geographic

Lego worked with the company National Geographic in 2017. They released a series of City jungle explorer sets. The companies joined forces again in 2020. They created the Deep Sea Explorers theme. These series were meant to get kids interested in the environment.

Deep Sea Explorers sets showcased many sea creatures, such as hammerhead sharks and manta rays.

A New Way to Play

In 2014, Lego released a series of sets featuring new technology. Builders could interact with the sets using augmented reality. The series was called Lego Fusion. A smartphone app added animation and sounds to the sets. Several Fusion sets fell within the City theme.

The Lego Group has released several interactive apps since 2014.

Water Police Detective Missions was one of three City Missions sets released in 2022.

A New Way to Build

City Missions launched in 2022. It introduced a new way to build and play with Lego sets. It was known as story-based building. Traditional building instructions were not used. Instead, builders downloaded an app with animated stories. The stories helped builders make the sets. They were also used to complete missions.

FUN FACT!

Minifigs with smartphones began appearing in City sets in the 2010s.

People can make their own Lego castles or build them from sets.

The First Castle

The first Lego castle was a photo in a Lego ideas book. The book was from 1960. The first castle set did not come out until ten years later. It was used to help sell cereal in the United Kingdom. People could get the set by mailing coupons from cereal boxes.

Legoland Castle

The Legoland Castle theme came out in 1978. It was inspired by Europe's medieval era (500–1500 CE). The first Legoland Castle was made of yellow bricks. The horses were also made of bricks. At first, castle sets were sold only in Europe. They were not sold in the United States until 1981.

The first Lego Castle set came with 14 minifigures.

Crusaders and Black Falcons

Legoland Castle was updated in 1984. New Lego pieces included horses, castle walls, and bows and arrows. Two rival factions were also introduced. One was the Crusaders. The other was the Black Falcons.

Each faction has a crest. The Black Falcons' crest is a falcon, *left*, while the Crusaders' crest is a lion.

The 1986 Guarded Inn set featured a female peasant, *right*.

Peasants

Legoland Castle first added peasant minifigures in the early 1980s. Peasants were poor farmers and workers. Sets such as the Supply Wagon, Blacksmith Shop, and Guarded Inn came with peasant minifigures.

The Forestmen crest was a brown male deer with black antlers on a green background.

Forestmen

The Forestmen faction was added in 1987. Forestmen were inspired by the legendary outlaw Robin Hood. Most sets included hidden tree forts. Minifigures wore green clothing. They also wore pointed hats.

The Forestmen faction ended in 1990. But a Forest Hideout set was rereleased in 2022.

Wolfpack

Wolfpack was a gang of outlaws. They were enemies of both the Forestmen and the knights. Wolfpack minifigures wore brown clothing. They also wore hoods. Between 1992 and 1993, only three sets were made. But the minifigs appeared in a few later castle sets.

The Wolfpack Renegades set came out in 1992.

Conflict and Violence

The Castle theme had many warring factions. Some sets introduced conflict and violence to the Lego universe. Kids can use minifigures in pretend fights. The Lego Group calls this conflict play. The company believes it can help children learn to deal with conflict in a healthy way.

Swords, spears, crossbows, and axes are some of the weapons featured in Castle sets.

Both the ghost and skeleton minifigure designs have changed over time.

Dead Minifigures

The first ghost minifigure released in 1990. It came with the King's Mountain Fortress set. The ghost glowed in the dark. It was the first glow-in-the-dark Lego piece. A skeleton minifig first appeared in Castle and Pirates sets in 1995. The minifig had been designed years earlier. But the Lego Group did not want to sell dead characters at that time.

Lego Weapons

Some Lego sets come with historic and futuristic weapons. But the Lego Group does not sell modern military-style weapons.

Majisto first appeared in the 1993 Wizard's Cart set.

Fantasy

Lego Castle entered a fantasy stage in 1993 with Dragon Masters. This faction included dragons. It also had a wizard named Majisto. Fright Knights came out soon after. This was a darker faction. It included black dragons, bats, and witches.

Royal Knights

Royal Knights was a knight faction. It lasted from 1995 to 1998. Royal Knights was the first to feature a king minifigure. New elements included a king's crown, armor, and a different sword design.

The 1995 Royal Knight's Castle included 11 minifigs.

The Lego Group released 17 sets under the Ninja subtheme.

Ninja

The Ninja subtheme ran from 1998 to 2000. It was based on Japanese history. In it, ninja assassins fought samurai warriors. Sets included castles, boats, and weapons.

Knights' Kingdom

Knights' Kingdom first released in 2000. It relaunched in 2004. Knights' Kingdom was the first set to have a complete royal family. The 2004 version included a story set. It took place in the fictional kingdom of Morcia. The story involved knights with superpowers. They fought the evil forces of the villain Vladek. This was the start of more action-packed Castle sets.

While Knights' Kingdom had traditional minifigs, it also had a series of larger action figures.

Lego Castle

A new Castle line ran from 2007 to 2009. It was different from previous Castle themes. It had more fantasy elements. Sets included dragons, wizards, and skeleton warriors.

General Bone, *pictured*, was a minifigure from The Final Joust set in the 2007 Castle line.

Kingdoms

The Castle theme was renamed Kingdoms in 2010. Kingdoms did not have most of Castle's fantasy elements. It centered on two rival knight factions. One was the Lion Kingdom. The other was the Dragon Kingdom.

The Kingdoms theme had many minifigures, including a court jester.

The Dragon Mountain set released in 2013. It featured a dragon guarding a treasure chest.

Lions and Dragons

Kingdoms was changed back to Castle in 2013. The new Castle theme mixed historical and fantasy elements. It also focused on the warring Lion Kingdom and Dragon Kingdom. But the two factions had updated colors and crests.

Nexo Knights

Nexo Knights was a futuristic Castle subtheme. It ran from 2016 to 2018. Nexo Knights was set in the fictional realm of Knighton. It included heroic knights. They battled evil forces to protect the realm. Many Nexo Knights sets were released. There was also an animated series.

King Halbert, the ruler of Knighton, was featured in a robotic battle suit in The King's Mech set.

Return to the Classics

Lego ended the Castle theme by the 2020s. But the company released some castle sets under the Icons theme. These large sets were meant for adults. They included the Medieval Blacksmith and the Medieval Town Square.

The instructions for building some retired Lego Castle sets can be found online.

The 2022 Lion Knights' Castle had Crusaders, Black Falcons, and Forestmen minifigs.

Lion Knights' Castle

The Lion Knights' Castle released in 2022. The set was created for Lego's ninetieth anniversary. It was inspired by sets from the 1980s. The Lion Knights' Castle was the largest Castle set at that time. It included 4,514 pieces. It also had 22 minifigures.

Dungeons & Dragons

In 2024, the Lego Group released a set based on the game Dungeons & Dragons. It also published a rule book that turned the set into a playable adventure game.

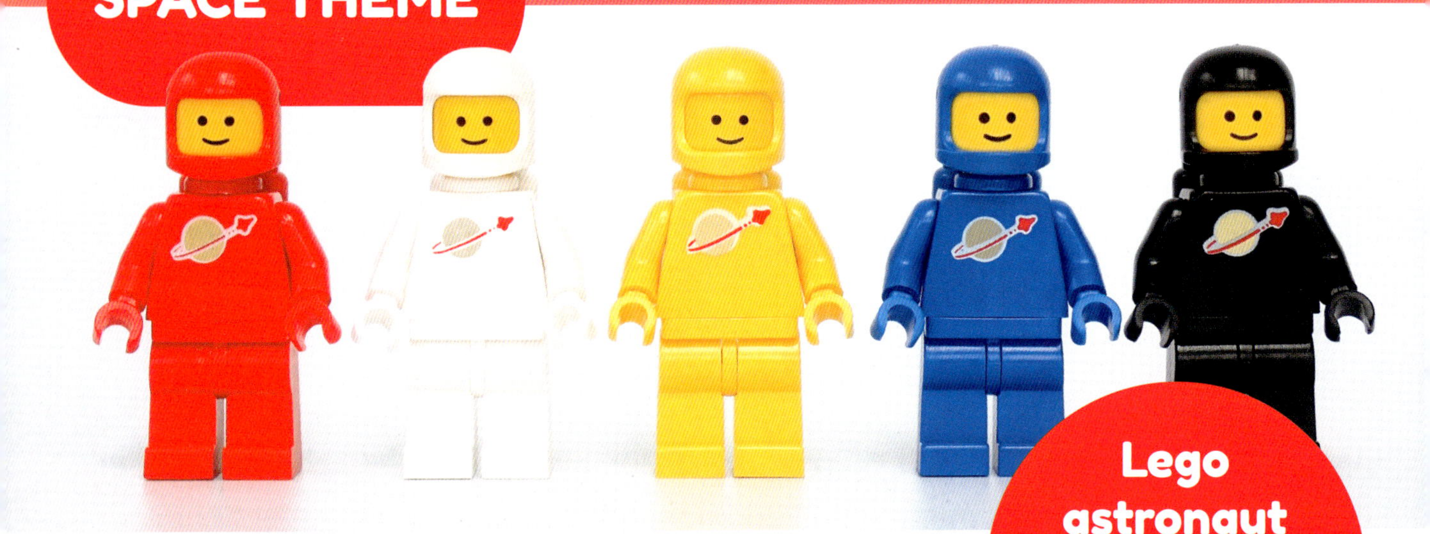

Lego astronaut minifigures first released in 1978.

The Space Race

An image of a rocket was shown on the cover of a 1964 Basic brick set. At the time, the United States and Soviet Union raced to create space technology. This was known as the space race. It got people interested in space.

Space Sets

The first Lego Space set was released in 1973. People could build a rocket and launchpad. A moon lander set came out two years later. These sets were based on real NASA spacecraft.

The first Lego Space set, called Rocket Base, did not come with any minifigures.

More than 300 sets were released under the Space theme.

Legoland Space

Legoland Space was one of the original three 1978 Lego themes. It included a mix of real space technology and science fiction. These sets focused on exploration.

Space Wars

Two rival space factions were introduced in 1987. They were Blacktron and Futuron. Blacktron was the outlaw faction of the universe. The Lego Group did not have weapons in sets at the time. Lego designers instead added radar dishes and antennas. Builders could easily imagine them as weapons.

Blacktron minifigs, *right*, had only black space suits. Futuron minifigs, *left*, came in yellow, blue, red, or black.

Space Police

Space Police launched in 1989. The faction worked with Futuron against Blacktron. Space Police vehicles often had jail cells built into them. The theme was updated in 1992 and 2009. The 2009 reboot included vehicles and criminal minifigures.

The 1992 Galactic Mediator was one of the largest Space Police ship sets.

All the sets in the M-Tron series were vehicles, so they did not have baseplates.

New Frontiers

More complex Lego bricks were made in the late 1980s and early 1990s. They allowed builders to create advanced space vehicles. Many had pieces that could detach and move into different positions. The 1990 M-Tron series used magnets to connect elements. It also had clear neon pieces.

FUN FACT!

The first Lego bricks with magnets were made in 1967.

The Robo-Guardian set from the Spyrius subtheme came out in 1994.

An Expanding Universe

Many space subthemes were released in the 1990s. Ice Planet 2002 took place on the frozen planet Krysto. The planet's location was great for launching rockets. Spyrius was a faction of spies and bandits. It used robots. The Exploriens theme was about space exploration.

First Contact

Lego UFO introduced the first alien minifigures in 1997. The aliens were known as Zotaxians. Several UFO sets used curved bricks to make flying saucers. Insectoids launched the next year. It featured aliens whose vehicles looked like insects.

FUN FACT!

UFO stands for unidentified flying object.

The Lego Group released several UFO sets in 1997, including the Cyber Saucer, *pictured*.

Alien Invasion

Alien Conquest hit stores in 2011. Unlike previous Space sets, Alien Conquest took place on Earth. It put humans against a race of alien invaders. Sets included alien flying saucers and humans from the Alien Defense Unit.

There were seven total sets for Alien Conquest. They all came out in 2011.

The Space Swarmer was one of the first Galaxy Squad sets.

The End of Space

Galaxy Squad came out in 2013. The subtheme saw humans defending the galaxy from a race of bug-like aliens. Lego ended its Space theme after Galaxy Squad. But the company still releases space sets under other themes. These include City, Technic, and Friends.

Early Expert Builder sets included a helicopter, a forklift, and a tractor.

Expert Builder

Expert Builder sets were released in 1977. They had gears and other special parts. Builders could make detailed working models.

Technic

Expert Builder sets were called Technical Sets in the United Kingdom. The line was renamed Technic in 1984. New Technic parts were added over the years. They allowed builds to become more complex.

Today, some of the most popular Lego Technic sets are cars.

Remote Control

Some Technic sets use batteries and electric motors. They may also have remote controls. The 2007 Motorized Bulldozer was the first remote-controlled Technic set. Control+ came out in 2019. Smartphones were used to control the vehicles.

The Remote-Controlled Stunt Racer set released in 2019.

The Technic Control Center came out in 1990. It was used to program Technic Control robots.

The Computer Age

Lego teamed up with the Massachusetts Institute of Technology in 1984. They designed a Technic robot. It was controlled by a computer. This resulted in a series called Lego Technic Control. It came out in 1986. The series was used in schools.

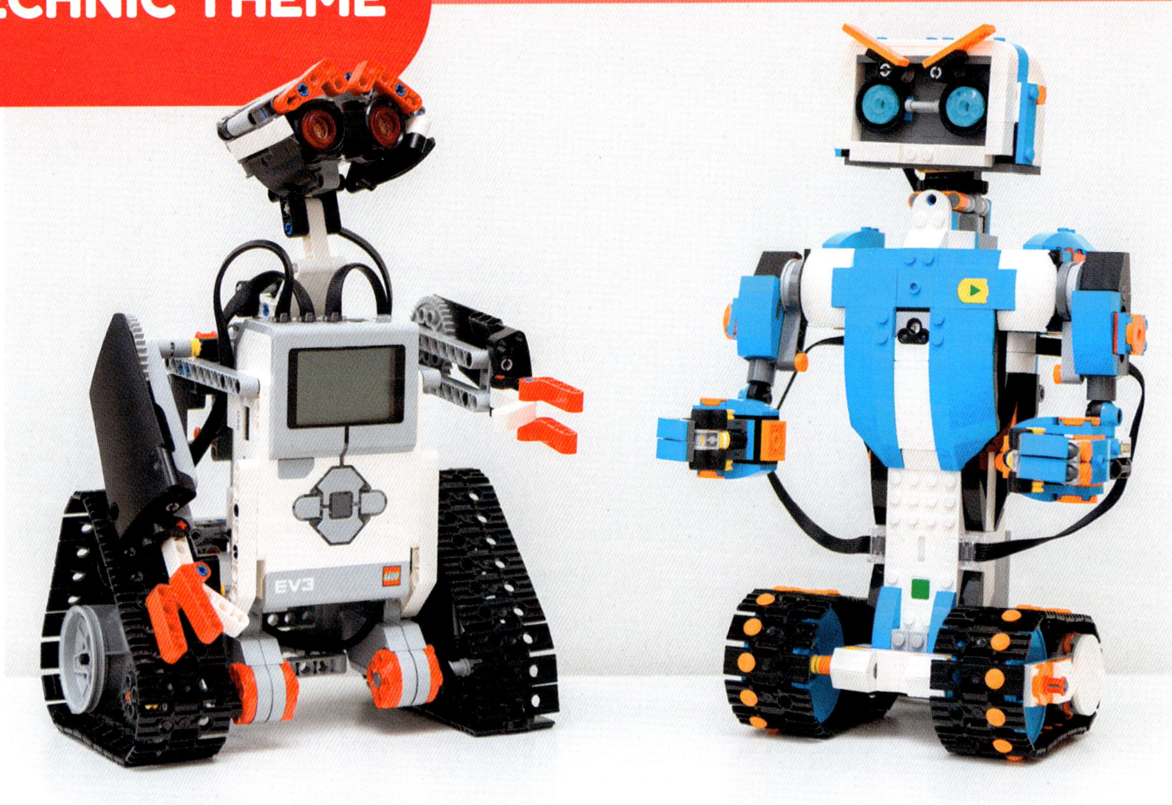

Older Lego robot sets, such as the 2013 Mindstorms EV3, *left*, sometimes had a programmable brick with a screen.

Lego Robots

Technic Control changed into Lego CyberMaster and Mindstorms. Both sets let builders make and program robots. Many schools used Mindstorms to teach STEM skills. Lego Boost came out in 2017. It made coding the robots easier.

Robot Inventor

The Mindstorms Robot Inventor set was released in 2020. Builders could make and program one of five different remote-controlled robots. An app provided people with instructions and activities.

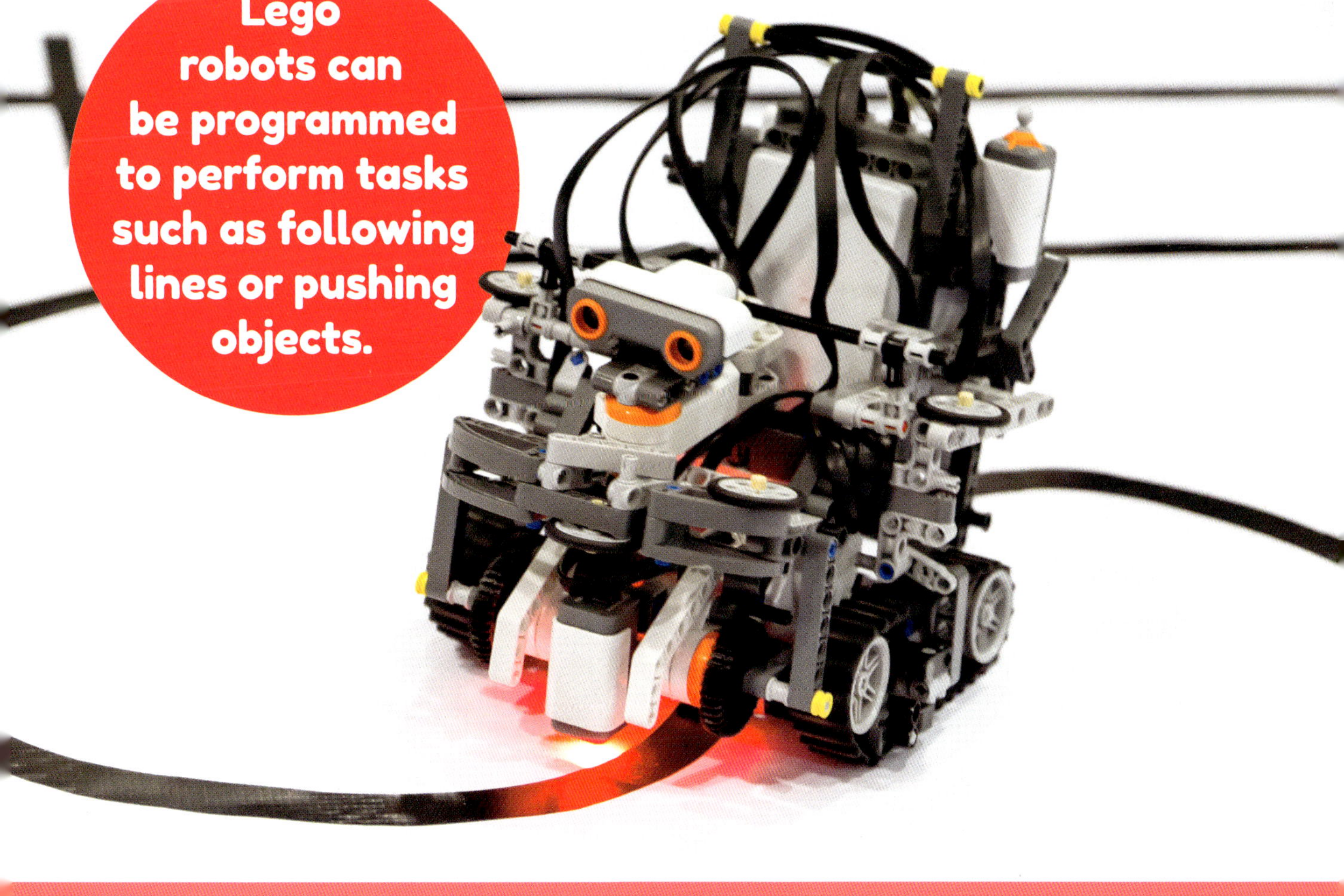

Lego robots can be programmed to perform tasks such as following lines or pushing objects.

Lego Education

Lego Education is a branch of the Lego Group. It promotes learning with Lego bricks. The organization provides Lego sets and lesson plans to schools.

Schools may have a robotics club or technology class where students can build and program Lego robots.

Lego Education SPIKE sets include brightly colored pieces.

Education SPIKE

Lego Education SPIKE sets are designed as teaching tools. Sets include Lego bricks, motors, and sensors. These are used for building and programming robots. Teachers can use the sets to help teach STEM subjects.

FIRST Lego League

The FIRST Lego League is a global robotics program. It hosts classes where kids use Lego bricks to learn about robotics. It also has robot-building competitions.

PIRATES THEME

The Black Seas Barracuda set was the first Lego Pirate ship. It released in 1989.

High Seas Adventure

Legoland Pirate System came out in 1989. Caribbean pirates battled Governor Broadside and his soldiers. The theme was based on piracy during the 1700s.

New Pieces

The Pirates theme introduced many new Lego pieces. These included monkeys, sharks, parrots, palm trees, and treasure chests. It also introduced new weapons. These included muskets, pistols, and cannons. Minifigures also had new face designs. Some faces had beards and eye patches.

FUN FACT!

Early Lego pirate ships came with cloth sails.

The Forbidden Island set was one of the first to release under the Pirates theme.

New Factions

In 1992, Governor Broadside's soldiers were renamed the Imperial Guard. The Islanders faction was added in 1994. It was based on traditional Pacific Island culture. The Imperial Armada was added two years later. It was modeled after Spanish soldiers from the 1500s and 1600s.

The back sail on the 1996 Imperial Armada ship could move up and down.

The 2010 Imperial Flagship, *left*, was the largest ship in the Pirates theme.

Reboots

New Pirates sets were released in 2009. They included pieces such as giant octopuses and updated minifigs. The Pirates theme came to an end in 2015. But some newer pirate sets were made under the Creator and Icons themes.

A McDonald's restaurant set came out in 1999.

Early Licenses

Lego gets permission to sell sets featuring popular brands. This is known as licensing. Sets using the Shell gas company name and logo go back to 1966. Other early licenses include Mercedes-Benz and the Maersk shipping company.

Star Wars

Lego licensed the Star Wars franchise in 1999. It became one of Lego's most popular themes. Many sets were updated over time. This was done as new bricks became available. The new bricks helped builds look more like the ships from the *Star Wars* movies.

Since 1999, more than 900 Lego Star Wars sets have been released.

Going Big

The Star Wars theme included some large builds. The 2017 *Millennium Falcon* was 33 inches (84 cm) long. It had 7,541 pieces. It was the largest Lego set at that time. The 2021 AT-AT set stood more than 2 feet (0.6 m) tall.

The 2016 Death Star was 16 inches (41 cm) wide and came with 23 minifigures.

Microfighter sets feature well-known ships and characters from throughout the Star Wars franchise.

Microscale

Lego started selling mini Star Wars sets in 2002. They were tiny ship models. In 2014, Lego launched Star Wars Microfighters. It was a series of small models. The models were made to fit minifigures.

Stud Shooters

The Lego stud shooter came out in 2014. It used a lever to shoot round Lego studs. One version of the shooter could be held by minifigures. Another could be added to ships and vehicles.

Builders could shoot baskets or score goals in some Lego Sports sets.

Lego Sports

Lego Sports ran from 2000 to 2007. Themes included soccer, basketball, and hockey. Some sets used real-life teams and leagues. They also featured minifigures of real sports players.

Soccer Stadiums

Lego has released a few soccer stadium sets. They are based on the stadiums of real professional soccer teams. These include Manchester United and Real Madrid.

The 2020 Old Trafford-Manchester United set was the first Lego soccer stadium.

Harry Potter

Lego launched its Harry Potter theme in 2001. More than 100 sets have been released since then. Popular sets included Hogwarts Castle, Hogwarts Express, and Quidditch Match.

The 2018 Hogwarts Castle is the biggest Harry Potter set, with 6,020 pieces.

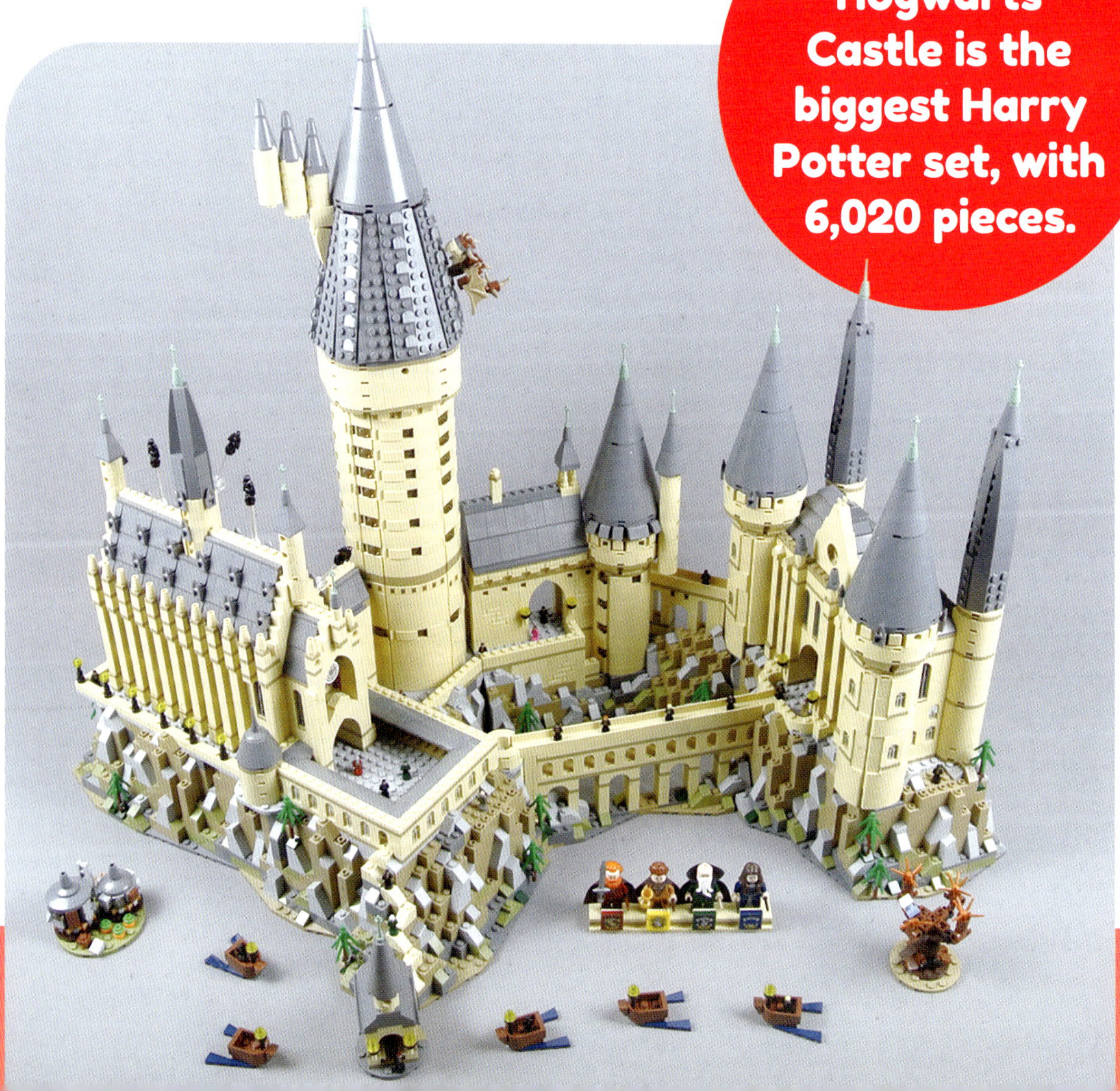

Jurassic Park

The first Jurassic Park sets were also released in 2001. They were known for their detailed dinosaur figures. Most had movable arms, legs, and jaws. The bodies had printed designs. The *Jurassic World* movies sparked their own theme in 2015.

Jurassic Park and Jurassic World sets often featured scenes from the films.

The first set from the Spider-Man theme was called Spider-Man's First Chase.

The First Superhero

The first licensed Lego superhero came out in 2002. It was Marvel's Spider-Man. The first sets were part of the Lego Studios theme. Studios was based on the movie industry. Some sets featured movie directors and camera operators. Spider-Man became its own theme in 2003. It later became a part of Lego's Marvel Super Heroes line.

Batman

DC's Batman was another early superhero license. Batman was its own Lego theme from 2006 to 2008. It then became part of the DC Super Heroes line. Popular sets included the Batmobile, the Bat Cave, and Arkham Asylum.

The *LEGO Batman Movie* released in 2017. The Lego Group sold sets based on the film.

Super Heroes

Lego Super Heroes began in 2012. The theme included characters from both the Marvel and DC universes. One of the largest sets was the 2023 Avengers Tower. It stood more than 36 inches (91 cm) tall. The set came with 31 minifigures.

Several superhero and villain minifigures exist in the Lego Super Heroes theme.

DC Super Hero Girls sets featured characters such as Wonder Woman, Batgirl, and Harley Quinn.

DC Super Hero Girls

DC Super Hero Girls focused on female DC superheroes and villains. The theme ran in 2017. It used classic Lego bricks. But it had mini-dolls instead of minifigures. Mini-dolls are taller than minifigs. They also look more realistic.

The Indiana Jones theme relaunched in 2023. Three sets were released, including Escape from the Lost Tomb, *back*.

Indiana Jones

In 2008, Lego decided to license another movie series. It was *Indiana Jones*. Sets featured classic scenes from the movies. They also had exciting names. These included Lost Tomb and Race for the Stolen Treasure.

The Lord of the Rings

Lego released sets based on The Lord of the Rings franchise in 2012. The sets featured well-known characters from the books and films.

The Rivendell set released in 2023. It included 6,167 pieces. That made it one of the largest sets ever.

The Lord of the Rings sets featured scenes and places from throughout all three films.

Pirates of the Caribbean

Lego has licensed many Disney films. A Pirates of the Caribbean theme launched in 2011. It was based on the popular movies about the adventures of pirate captain Jack Sparrow. Sets included tropical islands, pirate ships, and castles from the films.

The *Black Pearl* set, which is based on the ship in the *Pirates of the Caribbean* movies, released in 2011.

In 2015, the Lego Group launched three Disney Princess sets based on the movie *Frozen*.

Disney Princess

The Disney Princess theme launched in 2012. Sets focused on characters such as Snow White and Cinderella. The first sets were Duplo. More sets were added later to the Juniors line. These were for older kids. They used System bricks and mini-dolls.

Minecraft sets include creatures and places from the video games.

Video Games

Lego also makes sets based on video games. The game *Minecraft* has been an especially popular license. The first set came out in 2012. The theme includes minifigures with square heads. It also has blocky tools and weapons.

Super Mario

Nintendo's Super Mario was made into Lego form in 2020. Some sets are detailed models of characters. Others are playable levels from *Mario* games. The Mario figure interacts with the build. Screens on the figure display animations.

Sonic the Hedgehog

Sega's Sonic the Hedgehog was licensed in 2016. Sets feature levels from the *Sonic* video games.

Mario and Yoshi are some of the characters featured in Lego Super Mario sets.

Western

The Western theme included subjects often found in American Western movies. The first sets came out in 1996. They included a sheriff's office, a bank, and bandits. Sets featuring American Indians were added a year later.

The Fort Legoredo set first released in 1996 and was rereleased in 2002.

The Adventurers theme had four subthemes, which were Egypt, Dino Island, Orient Expedition, and Jungle.

Adventurers

The Adventurers theme focused on explorer Johnny Thunder and his friends. This theme ran from 1998 to 2003. Most Lego themes take place in fictional places. But Adventurers sets often featured real places. These included Egypt and the Amazon.

While the Vikings theme ended in 2007, a few Viking-related sets came out in the 2020s under the Creator theme.

Vikings

The Vikings theme is based on historical Norse explorer-warriors. Sets first came out in 2005. They featured ships, forts, and weapons similar to what real Vikings used. The sets also had creatures from Norse mythology. These included dragons and sea serpents.

Pharaoh's Quest

The Pharaoh's Quest theme started in 2011. It featured Professor Hale and adventurer Jake Raines's hunt for treasure. The treasure is inside ancient ruins. The ruins are filled with dangerous traps. They are also guarded by mummies, giant scorpions, and huge snakes. This theme was inspired by Egyptian history and mythology.

Mummy minifigs are found in many of the Pharaoh's Quest sets.

One of the original six Bionicle figures was Onua, the Toa of Earth.

Bionicle

Bionicle was one of the first Lego themes with a detailed storyline. It took place in the fictional Matoran universe. Its beings were part living and part robotic. They were called the Toa. The Toa fought to protect the universe. They had superpowers based on the elements air, fire, water, ice, earth, and stone.

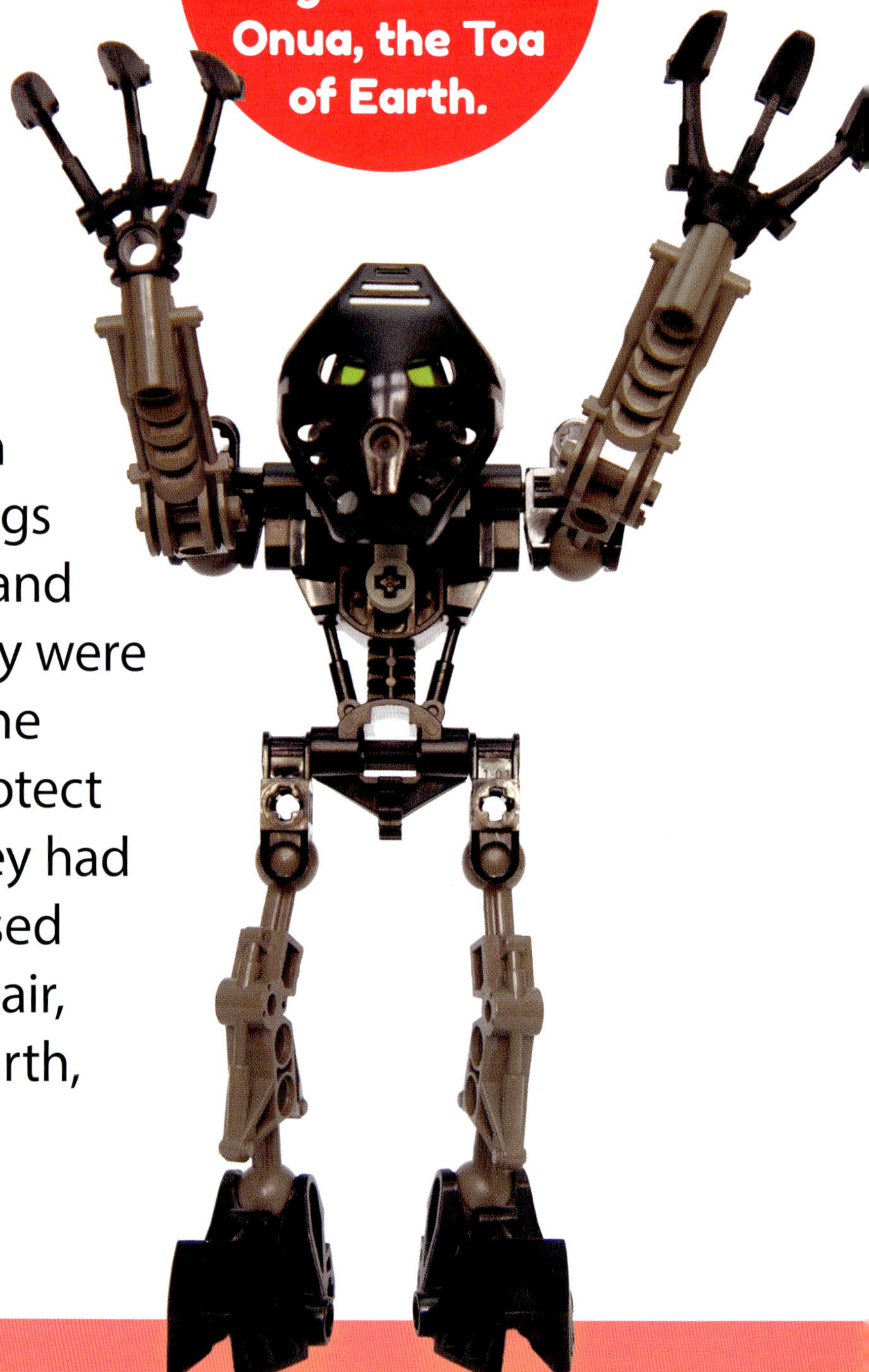

The 2015 Bionicle reboot featured a new storyline and characters.

A Successful Story

Bionicle sets featured action figures. The figures were made mostly of Technic parts. They could move their arms, legs, and heads. Bionicle ran from 2001 to 2010. It was rebooted from 2015 to 2016. Bionicle was one of the most popular Lego themes of all time.

FUN FACT!

Bionicle is a combination of the words *biological* and *chronicle*.

Mission Deep Sea sets were mainly underwater vehicles, such as the 2002 Alpha Team Navigator and ROV.

Alpha Team

The Alpha Team theme was about secret agents. The team fought to stop supervillain Ogel from taking over the world. The agents used high-tech vehicles and gear to save the day. This theme launched in 2001. Subthemes included Mission Deep Sea and Mission Deep Freeze.

FUN FACT!

Ogel is *Lego* spelled backward.

Agents

Alpha Team was followed by Agents in 2008. Agents was also based on a team of secret agents. They fought the mad scientist Dr. Inferno. Next came Ultra Agents in 2014. These secret agents battled several supervillains. Ultra Agents included two smartphone apps with interactive missions.

The Ultra Agents Ocean HQ set had 1,204 pieces and came with six minifigures.

Exo-Force

Futuristic robots turn against their human creators in Exo-Force. The two sides fight wearing suits of robotic battle armor. This theme was inspired by Japanese anime and manga stories. Exo-Force ran from 2006 to 2008.

***Mobile Suit Gundam* and *Robotech* were some of the Japanese series that inspired Exo-Force.**

Chima

The Legends of Chima theme was set in the fictional realm of Chima. The realm had warring tribes of animal-like beings. They fought over an energy source called Chi. The Legends of Chima had more than 100 sets between 2013 and 2015.

The Legends of Chima featured 20 animal tribes. These included the Lion Tribe, Eagle Tribe, and Crocodile Tribe.

Master Wu, *middle*, is a mentor to the ninjas in Ninjago.

Ninjago

A group of teenage ninjas fight to protect their realm in Ninjago. They are masters of the martial art Spinjitzu. They also ride dragons. These sets were released alongside a TV series beginning in 2011. Ninjago quickly became one of Lego's most popular themes.

The Ninjago Movie

The LEGO Ninjago Movie came out in 2017. In it, the ninjas suit up in robotic battle armor to defend Ninjago City. A series of related sets came out with the movie. These sets included Ninjago City and Garma Mecha Man. Another large set featured a flying ship called *Destiny's Bounty*.

The Garma Mecha Man set stood 11 inches (28 cm) tall and featured a shark blaster.

Monster Fighters

Monsters roamed Earth looking for magical stones in Lego Monster Fighters. A group of monster fighters stood in their way. Ten Monster Fighter sets were released in 2012. They featured haunted houses, castles, and creepy forests. Monster minifigs included vampires, zombies, ghosts, and mummies.

Each monster in Monster Fighters had its own set, such as The Zombies.

The Hidden Side boxes featured colorful artwork of the set rather than a photo.

The Hidden Side

Ghosts took over the fictional city of Newbury in The Hidden Side. Buildings and vehicles turned into monsters. A group of ghost hunters fought to return the city to normal. The theme came with an augmented reality app. It added audio and visual effects to sets when viewed on a screen. The theme ran from 2019 to 2020.

Belville

The Belville theme ran from 1994 to 2009. It was designed to appeal to girls. Sets featured doll-like figures. Their arms and legs were movable. Some came with cloth dresses.

Some Belville sets featured fantasy scenes. Others showed scenes of everyday life.

Friends

Lego Friends came out in 2012. This theme is also marketed to girls. The sets mostly have female characters. They also use mini-dolls. This theme features friends that live in the fictional Heartlake City. Each friend has different interests and hobbies.

More than 500 sets in the Friends theme have come out since 2012.

The 2015 Skyra's Mysterious Sky Castle was in the first wave of Elves sets released by Lego.

Elves

Lego Elves told a story of a girl named Emily. A portal brought her to a fantasy realm called Elvendale. The realm was home to elves, dragons, and goblins. The elves of Elvendale helped Emily find her way home. This theme was marketed toward girls. It also had mini-dolls. Elves ran from 2015 to 2018.

Dreamzzz

The 2023 Lego Dreamzzz theme is based on a TV show. The show is about a group of friends. They go into the magical Dream World. They battle the evil Nightmare King. Sets include colorful creatures and ships.

Several Dreamzzz sets have more than 1,000 pieces, including the 2023 Nightmare Shark Ship.

Lego Juniors

Juniors launched in 2014. Sets were meant for kids between four and seven. They used System bricks and minifigs. But these sets were simpler to build. Juniors used many Lego themes. These included City, Super Heroes, and Disney Princess. The theme was renamed Lego 4+ in 2018.

The Incredibles, Jurassic World, and Cars were some of the movie franchises used in the Juniors theme.

Some Dots sets have Lego bricks with letters or designs on them.

Lego Dots

The Dots theme uses Lego bricks to make craft projects. Projects include jewelry, boxes, and picture frames. People can also decorate patches with bricks. The patches can be sewn onto clothes or bags.

Modular buildings in the Creator Expert theme could be connected to one another.

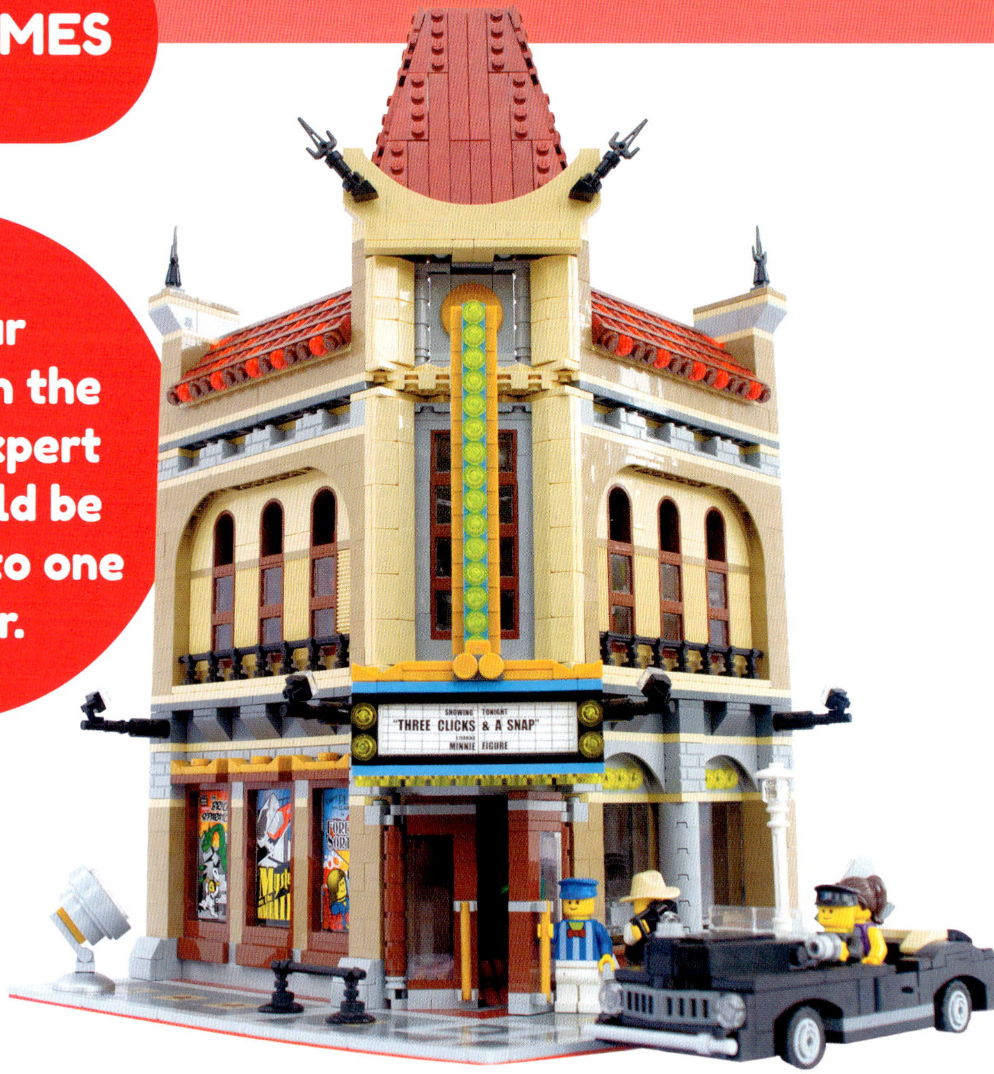

Creator Expert

Creator Expert ran from 2013 to 2020. It featured advanced builds. These were meant for adults. Sets included a wide range of subjects. Some were historic and modern vehicles. Others were flowers, town scenes, and video game characters.

Icons

Icons replaced Creator Expert in 2020. This theme is also meant for adults. Sets feature detailed model cars, movie scenes, and famous buildings. Icons also has several collections. Some of these are Botanical, Modular Buildings, and The Lord of the Rings.

AFOLs

Many adults collect and build Lego sets. They are known as AFOLs. This stands for Adult Fans of Legos. Some AFOLs share their builds online.

Botanical is one of the Lego Group's most popular collections.

BrickHeadz

Lego BrickHeadz are collectible figures. They are about 3 inches (8 cm) tall. These figures have very little detail. Most are characters from movies and video games. Some are pets. BrickHeadz started in 2016. It began with Marvel and DC sets.

The Lego Group has released BrickHeadz figures from many well-known franchises, including Disney, Star Wars, and Harry Potter.

The 2023 Great Wave set is based on a famous artwork by the same name created by artist Katsushika Hokusai in 1831.

Lego Art

Lego Art was introduced in 2020. The sets are pictures made of many small Lego bricks. Some recreate the work of famous artists. Others are inspired by movies and popular culture. Some have picture frames made of bricks.

The 2016 Yellow Submarine was an Ideas set based on a song by British rock band the Beatles.

Ideas

Ideas sets are designed by Lego fans. Fans can post images of their designs on the Lego Ideas website. Then other fans can vote on them. Sets with the most votes may be turned into official sets.

Idea Books

FUN FACT!

January 28 is International Lego Day.

Idea books contain images of unique Lego builds. These builds are not sold as sets. People can copy the builds. Or they can use them as inspiration. The books do not usually show instructions. Some have builds for multiple Lego themes. Others are specific to a single theme.

Lego idea books are great ways for builders to learn tips and tricks from others.

GLOSSARY

augmented reality
An experience that combines the real world with digital information.

coding
Writing instructions for computers to perform certain tasks.

faction
A small group of people within a larger group.

fantasy
Something that is purely imaginary.

franchise
A brand or business.

hollow
Empty inside.

imperial
Having to do with an empire.

license
A formal agreement that allows a company to use characters or images belonging to another company or person.

modular
Made up of separate parts that can be combined to form something.

mythology
A collection of tales belonging to a certain culture or religion.

outlaw
A person who has broken the law.

STEM
An acronym that stands for science, technology, engineering, and math.

subtheme
A smaller theme that is part of a larger one.

theme
The main story or subject.

TO LEARN MORE

More Books to Read

Hansen, Grace. *Lego*. Abdo, 2023.

Hugo, Simon. *The Big Book of Lego Facts*. DK, 2023.

Mooney, Carla. *Star Wars*. Abdo, 2026.

Online Resources

Booklinks
NONFICTION NETWORK
FREE! ONLINE NONFICTION RESOURCES

To learn more about Lego, please visit **abdobooklinks.com** or scan this QR code. These links are routinely monitored and updated to provide the most current information available.

INDEX

PHOTO CREDITS

Cover Photos: Adobe Stock, front (figure, Duplos, shelf), back; Iana Alter/Adobe Stock, front (Legos)

Interior Photos: iStockphoto, 1, 10 (classic minifigure), 10 (pirate), 30, 38, 55, 90, 96, 103; Shutterstock Images, 3, 4, 5, 9, 11 (bottom), 16, 20 (Lego), 23, 27 (bottom), 33 (top), 35, 48, 49 (bottom), 58, 59 (bottom), 72, 75, 77 (bottom), 82, 83, 85 (bottom), 89, 91, 92, 98, 99 (top), 113, 121 (top), 121 (bottom left), 122; David Mellis/Flickr, 6; Polfoto/Ritzau/Alamy, 7; Simon Robinson/Easy On The Eye/Alamy, 8, 18; Brickset, 10 (armless minifigure), 43, 57, 69, 84, 87, 88, 107, 114, 124; Andrey Arkusha/Shutterstock Images, 10 (Yoda); Jakub Porzycki/Anadolu Agency/Getty Images, 10 (basketball player); Ruslan Lytvyn/Shutterstock Images, 10 (mini-doll); Ekaterina Minaeva/Shutterstock Images, 10 (baby), 25, 32, 119; Donald Sylvester/Dads Brickshop, 11 (top), 29, 31 (top), 36, 64, 65, 78, 79, 80, 100, 101, 106; Red Line Editorial, 12, 20 (chart), 31 (bottom); Warner Bros./Photofest, 13; Jonathan Nackstrand/AFP/Getty Images, 14, 15; Wikimedia Commons, 17 (1934 logo); Sylvain Robin/Alamy, 17 (other logos); Niels Poulsen/Alamy, 19; Photo Media/ClassicStock/Archive Photos/Getty Images, 21; Yulia Vasilyeva/Shutterstock Images, 22; David Ross/Alamy, 24; Keith Homan/Shutterstock Images, 26, 93, 97, 116; Anders Sellin/Alamy, 27 (top), 61; myLAM/Alamy, 28; Fitria Ramli/Shutterstock Images, 33 (bottom); Ryan Gale, 34, 41, 44, 45, 46, 47, 51, 59 (top), 94, 102; Thiti Sukapan/Shutterstock Images, 37, 115; Darwin Strong, 39; Daniel Karmann/dpa/picture alliance/Getty Images, 40; John Hopkins/Alamy, 42; Stephen Fleming/Alamy, 49 (top), 52, 66; Michal Szymel/Alamy, 50; Schöning/ullstein bild/Getty Images, 53, 104; Flickr, 54, 68; Levent Konuk/Shutterstock Images, 56, 112; David A. Ross/Shutterstock Images, 60; Adobe Stock, 62; Patricia Phillips/Alamy, 63; John Stillwell/PA Images/Getty Images, 67; Wolfgang Spitzbart/Alamy, 70; Ivan Rendakov/Shutterstock Images, 71; Stephen Edmonds/Flickr, 73; Alesia Kan/Shutterstock Images, 74, 77 (top); John Carl D'Annibale/Albany Times Union/Hearst Newspapers/Getty Images, 76; Adam Purves/Flickr, 81; Burcu Ergin/Shutterstock Images, 85 (top); John Gichigi/Getty Images Sport/Getty Images, 86; Jonathan Brady/PA Images/Getty Images, 95; Colin Temple/Shutterstock Images, 99 (bottom); Sergey Kohl/Shutterstock Images, 105; Josh Hallett/Flickr, 108; Daniel Karmann/picture alliance/Getty Images, 109; Chris Wilson/Alamy, 110; Grzegorz Czapski/Shutterstock Images, 111, 118; Niall Carson/EMPPL PA Wire/PA Images/AP Images, 117; Tyrell Williams/Alamy, 120; Valeriia Lukashova/Shutterstock Images, 121 (bottom right); Bruno Ismael Silva Alves/Shutterstock Images, 123; Erman Gunes/Shutterstock Images, 125